How Do Insects Move?

Megan Kopp

 Crabtree Publishing Company
www.crabtreebooks.com

Author
Megan Kopp

Publishing plan research and development
Reagan Miller

Editor
Shirley Duke

Proofreader and indexer
Crystal Sikkens

Design
Samara Parent

Photo research
Tammy McGarr

Prepress technician
Tammy McGarr

Print and production coordinator
Margaret Amy Salter

Photographs
Thinkstock: Cover (girl); TOC; pgs 16, 17 21

All other images from Shutterstock

Library and Archives Canada Cataloguing in Publication

Kopp, Megan, author
How do insects move? / Megan Kopp.

(Insects close-up)
Includes index.
Issued in print and electronic formats.
ISBN 978-0-7787-1970-0 (bound).--ISBN 978-0-7787-1974-8 (pbk.).--
ISBN 978-1-4271-9036-9 (pdf).--ISBN 978-1-4271-9032-1 (html)

1. Insects--Physiology--Juvenile literature. I. Title.

QL467.2.K672 2015   j595.7   C2014-907829-3
C2014-907830-7

Library of Congress Cataloging-in-Publication Data

Kopp, Megan, author.
How do insects move? / Megan Kopp.
pages cm. -- (Insects close-up)
Includes index.
ISBN 978-0-7787-1970-0 (reinforced library binding) -- ISBN 978-0-7787-1974-8 (pbk.) -- ISBN 978-1-4271-9036-9 (electronic pdf) -- ISBN 978-1-4271-9032-1 (electronic html)
1. Animal locomotion--Juvenile literature. 2. Insects--Anatomy--Juvenile literature. 3. Insects--Behavior--Juvenile literature. I. Title.

QP301.K629 2015
595.715'7--dc23
2014045635

Crabtree Publishing Company

Printed in Canada/042015/BF20150203

www.crabtreebooks.com   1-800-387-7650

Published in Canada
Crabtree Publishing
616 Welland Ave.
St. Catharines, Ontario
L2M 5V6

Published in the United States
Crabtree Publishing
PMB 59051
350 Fifth Avenue, 59th Floor
New York, New York 10118

Published in the United Kingdom
Crabtree Publishing
Maritime House
Basin Road North, Hove
BN41 1WR

Published in Australia
Crabtree Publishing
3 Charles Street
Coburg North
VIC 3058

Contents

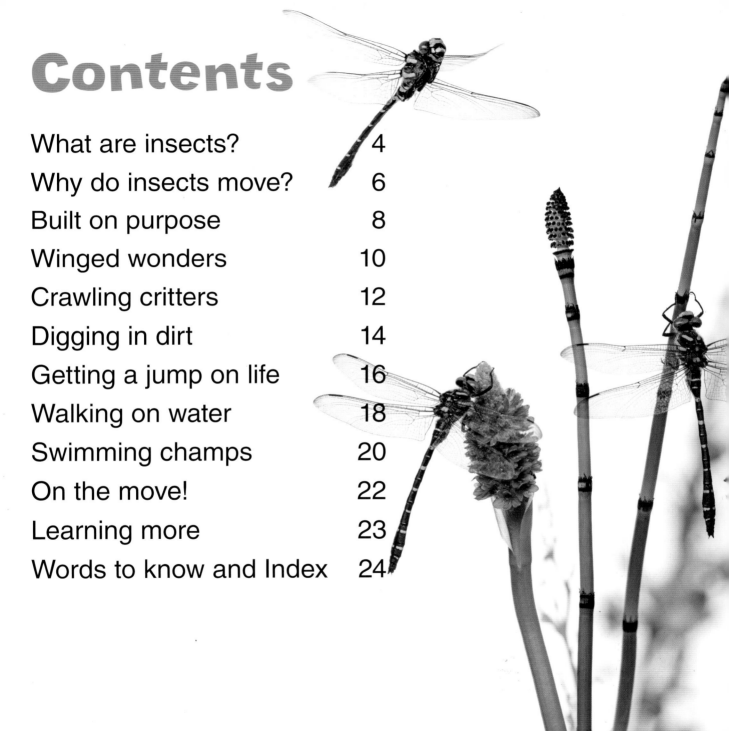

What are insects?

Insects are animals without backbones. They have a hard, shell-like skeleton that covers the outside of their body. This is called an **exoskeleton**. An insect's body is made up of three parts. There is a head at one end, a **thorax** in the middle, and an **abdomen** at the other end.

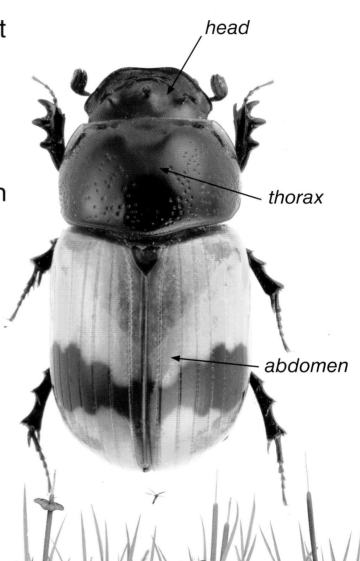

head

thorax

abdomen

Sharing the same parts

All insects have six legs that bend where they meet at the **joint**. Their legs come in many shapes and sizes. Insect legs are built for how the insect moves. Insects also have two **antennae** on their heads. Antennae are sometimes called feelers. Almost all insects have four wings.

Some legs match an insect's body.

Grasshoppers are built for jumping.

wings

antennae

legs

Butterflies use their antennae for smelling.

Why do insects move?

All living things move. Some living things can move on their own. Insects move in many ways. Crickets hop. Bumblebees fly. Caterpillars crawl. Do you run or walk away if a baseball is coming right at you? When you are excited, do you jump up and down or stand still? Like people, insects move for many different reasons.

Many insects move to avoid being eaten.

On the move!

Insects move to explore their **environment**. They move to look for food, shelter, or to find a mate. Sometimes insects move to keep from being eaten by **predators**. Insects also move to **communicate** with other insects.

Insects, such as these wasps, move to build their homes.

Built on purpose

An insect's body is built for how it moves. Grasshoppers have long legs with powerful muscles for jumping. Water beetles use their legs to row in water. Stiff hairs on their legs help them swim.

Great diving beetle

stiff hairs on back legs

Grasshoppers can jump quickly to avoid predators.

Move along!

An insect's six legs are jointed to allow for extra movement. Have you ever watched a fly as it walks? It moves three legs at a time. Flies move the front and back leg on one side of its body and the middle leg on the other. This way it is always solid on the ground.

What do you think?

Most insects have four wings. How do you think the wings help them move?

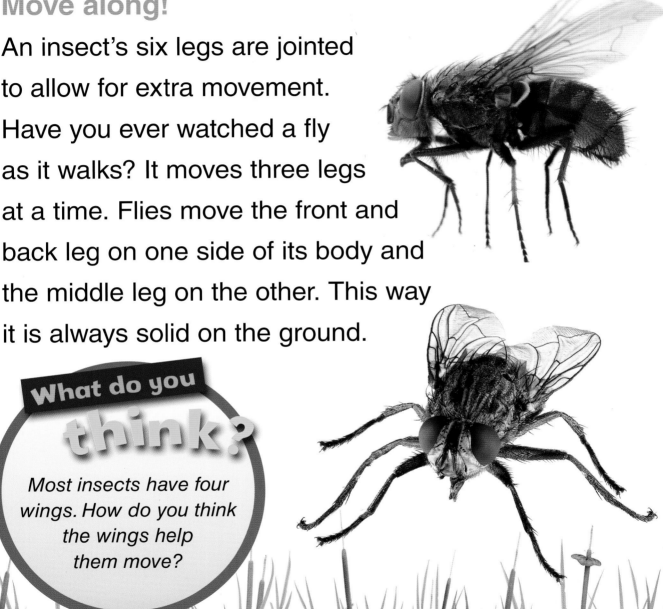

9

Winged wonders

Insects were the first living things to fly. Most insect **species** have two pairs of wings. Insect wings are thin but strong. Insects use their wings to **hover**, fly backward, or fly forward. Flight helps insects move from place to place to find food. Flying also helps insects escape predators.

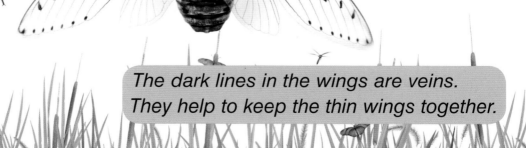

The dark lines in the wings are veins. They help to keep the thin wings together.

Flight of fancy

The wings of butterflies and moths are covered with colored scales. The outer wings of beetles are hard and shell-like. They fit over the thin, inner wings to protect them. Dragonfly wings don't fold up. They are always ready to move fast. Mosquitoes only have one pair of wings.

Ladybugs must lift their outer wings before flying.

Butterfly wings often have colorful patterns.

Crawling critters

Cockroaches are winged insects that crawl instead of fly. Their bodies allow them to crawl very fast. A cockroach can crawl 50 times the length of its body in one second. Cheetahs are the fastest **mammals** on land. Cockroaches move at three times the speed of cheetahs.

Cockroaches are low to the ground, have flat bodies, and long back legs. These features allow them to crawl quickly.

Pincer protection

Earwigs are winged insects that also prefer to crawl instead of fly. They have pincers, or curved claws, on the end of their abdomen that they use for protection. Earwigs stay hidden during the day and hunt for food at night.

Some insects crawl away and hide under fallen leaves.

pincers

earwig

What do you think?

Earwigs have pincers on their abdomen. Name the other two sections of their bodies.

Digging in dirt

Some insects live underground. Mole crickets dig into dirt to create **burrows**. These crickets don't need to move fast because there are not as many predators underground. Adult mole crickets have wings that are much smaller than their bodies. Small wings make them clumsy in the air when they fly.

Mole crickets do not fly very often.

Built for life underground

Mole crickets have **adapted** to their environment. They have large, powerful front legs used for digging. Mole crickets have tiny hairs along their body and legs. These hairs help to keep the soil from sticking to the insect's body.

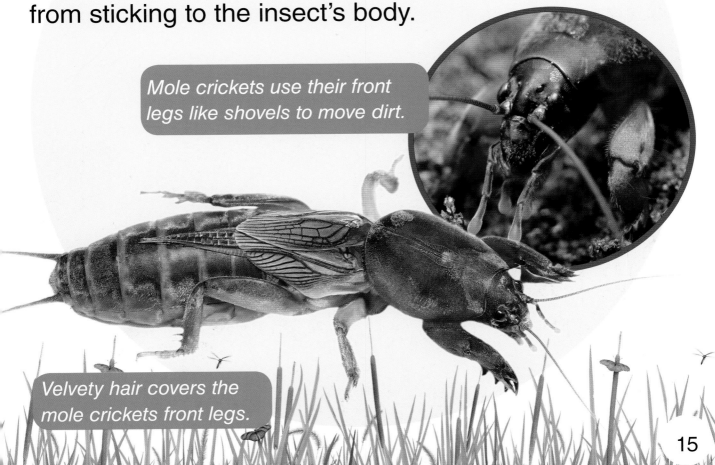

Mole crickets use their front legs like shovels to move dirt.

Velvety hair covers the mole crickets front legs.

Getting a jump on life

Being able to jump is helpful in the insect world. Jumping insects can spring away from something that wants to eat them. They can also jump toward something they want to eat! Crickets, fleas, and leafhoppers are all star jumpers.

Leafhoppers eat sap from leaves. They jump from leaf to leaf for food.

Tiny fleas can jump over 80 times their own height.

Grasshopper getaway

Grasshoppers can walk and fly, but they prefer to jump away from danger. Grasshoppers have powerful back legs. The upper part of the leg is all muscle. This muscle is 10 times more powerful than the strongest human muscle. The lower part of the grasshopper's leg is long. This helps push the insect forward.

What do you think?

Grasshoppers and mole crickets both have powerful legs. What are some of the differences between them?

A grasshopper can jump 20 times the length of its body.

Walking on water

You can skate on water when it is frozen. Water striders skate on water during the middle of summer. Striders are skinny insects with long legs. They have fine hairs on their feet. These hairs stop the strider's legs from breaking through the water surface. This allows them to skate across the top of a calm pond or lake.

A water strider's long legs and light body allow it to skate across the top of a calm pond or lake.

Liquid steps

There are very few insect species that can walk on water. This means there is little need to fight for food. Water striders feed on spiders and insects that land on the water surface.

Water striders use their short front legs for grabbing food.

Swimming champs

Like most insects, water boatmen and backswimmers have wings and can fly. But these two insects spend most of their lives underwater. Both species have adapted for life underwater. They carry a bubble of air with them. It allows them to breathe underwater.

Water boatmen trap air bubbles around their body and under their wings.

Alike but not the same

Water boatmen and backswimmers are often mistaken for each other. The rear legs of both insects are flat and covered with rows of **bristles**, or stiff hairs. They use their legs like paddles to row through the water. The main difference between the two insects is that backswimmers swim on their backs.

What do you think?

Name another insect that rows through the water with back legs covered in stiff hairs.

backswimmer

On the move!

Make a poster to share what you have learned about how insects move with your family and friends. On a piece of paper, draw a picture of a park. You can add grass, trees, and a stream. Then, draw or cut out pictures of different kinds of insects jumping, crawling, swimming, flying, and digging. Place the pictures on the poster and write how each insect moves under its picture.

Learning more

Books

Lawton, Caroline. *Bugs A to Z*. Scholastic Paperbacks, 2011.

Llewellyn, Claire. *The Best Book of Bugs*. Kingfisher Press, 2005.

Murawski, Darlyne & Nancy Honovich. *Ultimate Bugopedia: The Most Complete Bug Reference Ever*. National Geographic Children's Books, 2013.

Websites

The Bug Chicks: How Insects Move
http://thebugchicks.com/uncategorized/how-insects-move/

University of Kentucky Entomology for Kids
www.uky.edu/Agriculture/Entomology/ythfacts/allyr/ythfacts.htm

Backyard Insects
www.backyardnature.net/2insect.htm

Biokids: Critter Catalogue: Grasshoppers and relatives
www.biokids.umich.edu/critters/Orthoptera

Words to know

Note: Some **boldfaced** words are defined where they appear in the book.

adapt (uh-DAPT) verb To change over a long time

antennae (an-TEN-ee) noun Feelers that help insects sense the world around them

burrows (BUR-ohs) noun Tunnels or holes dug into the ground

communicate (kuh-MYOO-ni-kate) verb To share information, ideas, or feelings

environment (en-VYE-ruhn-muhnt) noun The natural surroundings of living things

hover (HUHV-ur) verb To remain in one place in the air

joint (JOINT) noun A place where two or more things meet or come together

mammal (MAM-uh-l) noun A warm-blooded animal that has a backbone and gives birth to live young

predators (PRED-uh-ters) noun Animals that hunt other animals for food

species (SPEE-sheez) noun A group of like animals

A noun is a person, place, or thing.
A verb is an action word that tells you what someone or something does.

Index